Aut
LE

MODERN ERAS
·UNCOVERED·
the early
1990s
to
2001

From the World Wide Web to September 11

Pat Levy and Sean Sheehan

Raintree

www.raintreepublishers.co.uk
Visit our website to find out more information about **Raintree** books.

To order:
☎ Phone 44 (0) 1865 888113
▤ Send a fax to 44 (0) 1865 314091
🖳 Visit the Raintree Bookshop at **www.raintreepublishers.co.uk** to browse our catalogue and order online.

First published in Great Britain by Raintree, Halley Court, Jordan Hill, Oxford, OX2 8EJ, part of Harcourt Education.
Raintree is a registered trademark of Harcourt Education Ltd.

Editorial: Melanie Copland and Lucy Beevor
Design: Michelle Lisseter and Bridge Creative Services Ltd
Picture Research: Mica Brancic and Ginny Stroud Lewis
Production: Duncan Gilbert

Originated by Chroma Graphics (Overseas) Pte. Ltd
Printed and bound in China by South China Printing Company

ISBN 1 844 43958 5
10 09 08 07 06
10 9 8 7 6 5 4 3 2 1

British Library Cataloguing in Publication Data
Levy, Patricia
From the World Wide Web to September 11.
– (Modern Eras Uncovered)
909.8'29
A full catalogue record for this book is available from the British Library.

Acknowledgements
Alamy p. **25**; Alamy/ImageState p. **23**; ARDEA p. **43**; Associated Press pp. **4, 14, 17, 31**; Corbis/Bernd Obermann p. **48**; Corbis/Bill Varie p. **6**; Corbis/Colin McPherson p. **8**; Corbis/eph Sohm; ChromoSohm Inc. p. **41**; Corbis/Howard Davies p. **42**; Corbis/Jose Fuste Raga p. **24**; Corbis/Massimo Mastrorillo p. **40**; Corbis/Peter Turnley pp. **12, 13, 18, 32, 33**; Corbis/Reuters pp. **16, 20, 28, 29, 37, 38, 44, 45, 47, 49**; Corbis/SABA/David Butow p. **5**; Corbis/Sygma/Keerle, Georges De p. **35**; Getty p. **19**; Metro Pictures, courtesy of the artist p. **22**; Rex pp. **15, 39, 46**; Science Photo Library/James King-Holmes p. **9**; Science Photo Library/Martin Bond p. **10**; Science Photo Library/Peter Menzel p. **11**; The Advertising Archive pp. **7, 26**; Virginia Stroud-Lewis p. **27**.

Cover photograph (top) reproduced with permission of Corbis, and photograph (bottom) reproduced with permission of Corbis/Reuters.

Every effort has been made to contact copyright holders of any material reproduced in this book. Any omissions will be rectified in subsequent printings if notice is given to the publishers.

The paper used to print this book comes from sustainable resources.

CONTENTS

Any words appearing in the text in bold, **like this**, are explained in the glossary.

AN END OF HISTORY?

The two events that frame the years between the early 1990s and 2001 are the development of the World Wide Web and the attacks on New York and Washington, D.C. in the United States on September 11. These were both unthinkable at the beginning of the 20th century. The computer technology that made the World Wide Web possible could not even have been imagined in 1900. The Wright brothers had made the first successful flight of a powered aircraft in 1903, but the idea of a super-fast airplane carrying hundreds of passengers was a distant dream. The idea that such aircraft might be hijacked and deliberately flown into 110-storey buildings, killing almost 3,000 people, was unimaginable.

The **Cold War**, the rivalry between the United States and the **USSR**, was over and this made the 1990s very different from the previous four decades. The threat of a nuclear war between the Cold War **superpowers** had disappeared and it seemed as if the world might become a safer place than ever before. Unfortunately, this is not what happened. New conflicts emerged and a number of old problems were still around.

East and West Berliners finally meet again during the collapse of the Berlin Wall in 1989, which signalled the end of the Cold War.

The end of the Cold War also made the United States more powerful than ever before. Not everyone agreed on how this power should be used. It was thought of as a threat in some **Islamic** societies, because US power was seen as the face of a new **empire** that wanted to control the world. From another point of view, US power represented values, such as individual freedom, which would bring progress and prosperity to all. The consequences of this difference of opinion became far clearer after the events of September 11, 2001.

Carnival against capitalism

In the United States in November 1999, around 75,000 people gathered to protest and demonstrate in the city of Seattle. From their point of view, much of the inequality around the world was due to **capitalism**. This is the system of private ownership of wealth that the **economies** of most countries in the world are based upon. Unlike the Cold War conflict (between **communism** and capitalism), the anti-capitalist protestors wanted peaceful change. As well as Seattle, protests also took place in European cities and in India.

People gather to demonstrate against the inequality of wealth in the world, in Seattle, Washington, United States, November 1999.

As the 1990s began most homes in the UK did not have a computer. The few that did had computers that could not permanently store information. Schools had been using UK-designed computers called Acorn BBCs that did not use a system like Microsoft Windows. By the 1990s, these computers were being replaced by personal computers (PCs). Few people had any idea of how important computers would become over the following years, or how quickly email and the World Wide Web would become an essential part of their lives.

During the 1990s, telephone lines were used to link one computer system to another, both within a country and internationally. As computers became cheaper to buy, people began to use PCs at home to write emails and eventually to surf the **Internet**.

The World Wide Web

The Internet was started in 1969 by the US military. At first it was just a small number of computers linked to one another by a telephone line. In 1986, this idea was taken up by universities that wanted to share information. Eventually, the Internet became available to people with their own PCs who wanted to access the information available in university systems through the use of web browsers. A web browser is a program that allows you to search for and display web pages from the Internet.

The Internet became popular as a way of searching for information as well as a way of communicating. Later on in the 1990s the Internet was to become a vital part of most businesses. The system that allowed computer users to search for information, as well as send and receive it, became known as the World Wide Web. The initials www became the standard **prefix** of most websites.

An advert for the hugely successful Internet business e-bay, from the 1990s.

going, going, gone-on-line.

Buy

Sell

PDA's
MP3 Players
DVD's
In-Car Entertainment
Gaming Consoles
Widescreen TV's
Mobile Internet
Mini Discs
Digital Cameras
Home Cinema
HiFi's
Arcade Machines

You can buy and sell anything on eBay. **ebaY**.CO.UK

Rapid advances

In the 1990s, change in technology was moving so quickly that electronic products could go out of date and become useless within a few years or even months of their development. One of the major new inventions of the late 1980s had been the facsimile (fax) machine, which could send a copy of printed text and pictures through telephone lines. Millions were sold all around the world. The development of email technology – sending text and pictures from one computer to another using telephone lines – made the fax machine largely unnecessary. They are still used, but less and less so.

Computers with already out-of-date technology are simply thrown away.

Who owns the Internet?

The Internet does not have national borders. Anyone can create a website that is then open to everyone around the world. No one really owns the Internet and anyone who has the right equipment, and an Internet connection, can use it. However, there are some ways of controlling the Internet. Companies called service providers enable people to connect to the Internet and this service can be controlled by governments. Computer users in China, for example, will find a blank page if they use the Internet to try to find information that the Chinese government does not want them to have.

Cloning

Cloning means making an identical, or exact, copy of a living cell, gene, or creature. Until the 1990s this was not possible, but in 1996 the first **clone** was born. She was a sheep called Dolly.

Bring in the clones

Soon, Dolly was followed by more cloned animals: a monkey and piglets in 2000, and cows and a cat in 2001. These animals, however, came at a high cost. Dolly was the 277th attempt to clone a sheep, and 9,000 attempts were made before cows were successfully cloned. Also, few of the animals survived for long. Dolly developed a lung disease and had to be put to sleep.

To make a clone, or copy, of an animal, you need a donor animal. This is the animal that is copied, and whose **cells** are used. When Dolly was born, her cells were the same age as those of the donor animal, instead of being new and young. This went against the theory that a cloned animal would be created as if from birth. Even though the failure rate was high and the experiments cost a lot of money, the benefits of developing a successful cloning method were huge. Cloning could be used to cure many diseases that were thought incurable.

Dolly, the world's first cloned living creature, was born in 1996 in Edinburgh, Scotland.

Human cloning?

The birth of Dolly raised the issue of human cloning. Some think this is a good idea, but others are strongly against it. Human egg cells can develop into any kind of cell: kidney, heart, liver, and even brain cells. If a person became very ill, a cloned egg cell containing their **DNA** could be grown into a replacement **organ** for them. This could help to cure some killer diseases. Other doctors think that cloning could be a way of giving babies to **infertile** couples. Other plans for cloning seem more like ideas from science-fiction stories. The most startling idea is that a whole body could be grown, but without a brain. This would allow the brain of a dying person to be inserted into a new version of their body – giving them a new life.

Objections

Many people object to these ideas for different reasons. People might choose to have children made from clones of themselves. This, it is argued, is against the way in which every life is a new and different life. Others object because they say the benefits of clone research will only become available to those who are rich. The cost of all the research could instead be devoted to treating and curing diseases that affect millions of people, such as **AIDS**.

At the moment, both the UK and the United States only allow clone research if it is about finding ways to cure diseases. Many doctors think, though, that it is only a matter of time before human cloning takes place.

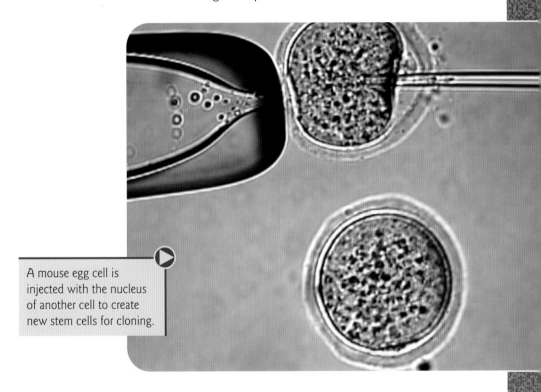

A mouse egg cell is injected with the nucleus of another cell to create new stem cells for cloning.

How is it done?

Each cell in our bodies contains deoxyribonucleic acid (DNA). Except for a few plants (and identical twins) no two living things have the same DNA. When a baby is made, DNA from the mother mixes with DNA from the father to make a new, completely original person with new DNA. In the technology that created Dolly, the nucleus (centre) of a sheep's egg cell was removed and the nucleus of another cell from a donor sheep was put in its place. The baby sheep that developed had the same DNA as the donor sheep, so it was not a new, original sheep.

The Human Genome Project

Genes are the long strands of DNA that decide what all living things will be like. DNA decides, for example, the colour of your hair, your height, whether you may suffer from some kind of **inherited** disease or condition. Discovering and identifying all the human genes would be like finding a set of instructions for how to build a human. A project to map and identify every gene, the Human Genome Project, began in 1990 by agreement between China, France, Germany, Japan, the United States, and the UK.

The consequences

All the human genes discovered so far have now been mapped out. This means that each of these 30,000 identified genes can be studied to find out what they do in the human body and if they are linked to any disease or illness. Eventually, scientists hope to discover the purpose of every human gene. If they can do this, it will allow a gene to be slightly changed, or replaced. This could remove anything that is seen as an imperfection, such as a disease or **birth defect**. It may even be possible, in the future, to remove any inherited diseases or birth defects before the baby is even born.

Genetic engineering

The ability to change, or modify, genes artificially is called genetic engineering. Some plants and animals have already been genetically engineered. Farm crops such as soya and corn have been developed to be resistant to chemicals sprayed on to them to kill pests. This means the chemicals will kill the pests, but leave the crops unharmed.

This seems like a good idea, and it has been done, but there may be dangers. No one is quite sure if genetically engineered crops will develop other characteristics. For example, they may also become resistant to chemicals. This means that they may not be able to be controlled and they could start growing all over the countryside. Other characteristics could also be a serious problem if they are changes that will be harmful to other forms of life.

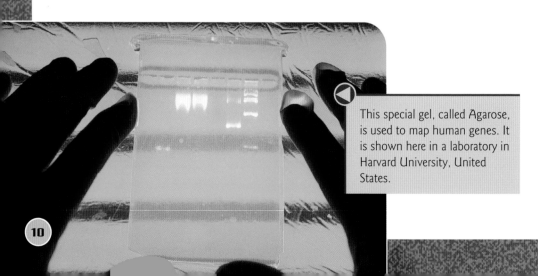

This special gel, called Agarose, is used to map human genes. It is shown here in a laboratory in Harvard University, United States.

GM foods

Genetically modified (GM) foods have caused a lot of debate in recent years. Some people think it is fine to buy and eat GM foods, whereas others are more worried about the side-effects of eating modified foods. So far there is no evidence of GM foods being harmful to humans. However, the rules for their testing are much less strict than those governing medical testing, for instance.

Environmental groups, such as Greenpeace, claim that genetic engineering is moving too quickly because there has not been enough testing on these products, and some companies just want to make lots of money very quickly. In some countries, but not all, food products have to show on their labels if they are genetically modified (GM) or not, so that people know what they are buying, and can choose by themselves.

Imagine what genetically modified (GM) tomatoes would look like if they were to have warning labels!

DNA fingerprints

In the 1980s, scientists found a way to identify a person's DNA. Since each person's DNA is **unique** and is present in cells in their body, a tiny piece of hair or a single skin cell is enough for scientists to work out the DNA of any person. Police now use this technology to help them catch criminals.

OLD PROBLEMS, NEW SOLUTIONS

In the UK, the **Conservative** government had been in power since 1979 and many people were surprised when they won again in the general election of 1992. When Tony Blair became the new leader of the Labour party he set about creating "New Labour," determined to win the next election. Blair and his supporters thought that in order to win they should present themselves as a safe and reliable party. They promised to make the UK a fairer and less greedy society. In doing this, New Labour hoped to appeal to a wide variety of voters. In the 1997 election, New Labour won by a huge majority and formed a new government.

Righting wrongs in South Africa

Election day

In 1994, an extraordinary election took place in South Africa. There had been elections there before, but only white people – 10 per cent of the population – could vote. This was all part of the racist system of **apartheid**. Now, every adult had the right to vote and between 26 and 29 April, 20 million black South Africans queued up to elect the country's first **democratic** government.

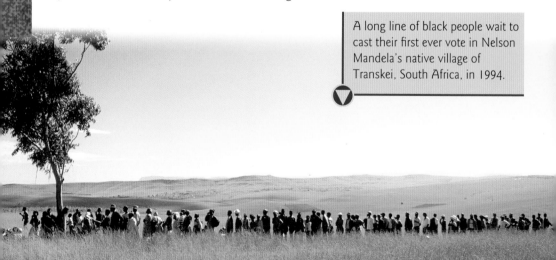

A long line of black people wait to cast their first ever vote in Nelson Mandela's native village of Transkei, South Africa, in 1994.

The world watched the election on television surprised that such a racist society had changed so much. There had been some violence by white racists, including two car bombs that exploded killing nineteen people, but they could not stop the election of a black government.

Mandela and Mbeki

The African National Congress (ANC) formed the new South African government. The ANC was the main party representing black people, and its leader, Nelson Mandela, became president of South Africa. White leaders had kept Mandela in prison for 26 years, but he was still a very strong and popular leader. As president, Mandela set about creating work for black people and improving their standard of living.

Under apartheid black South Africans had suffered in all sorts of ways, from attending poor schools to living in slum housing, and there was a lot to do. Black people did not trust white politicians and in the next election, in 1997, the ANC won more votes than before. Nelson Mandela retired and Thabo Mbeki became president.

Supporters of Nelson Mandela and the ANC gather at a campaign rally before South Africa's first democratic election on 27 April 1994, now known as "Freedom Day."

Anastaia Ncgobo remembers

Anastaia Ncgobo was one of the millions of ordinary black South Africans who voted in 1994 for a peaceful future, while still remembering the violent past:

"I am here remembering all the people who suffered for this day: all of the children who were killed; Mr Mandela going to prison; the young men who went into exile. Oh, it's too much, too much suffering has happened for this day. But in the end we know it was worth it. To be here and going to vote. I never thought I would see it in my lifetime."

(FROM THE BONDAGE OF FEAR BY FERGAL KEANE)

Truth and reconciliation

Steve Biko, a black South African leader in the late 1970s who had been beaten to death by the police, was one of the many victims of apartheid. His family wanted his murderers punished. The white government, before agreeing to the 1994 multi-racial election, had been promised by the ANC that white people would not be **prosecuted** for what had happened in the past. What could be done to keep this promise while also being fair to the families of people like Steve Biko?

Forgiving, not forgetting

The solution was a Truth and Reconciliation Commission (TRC). This would examine, in public, cases of injustice under apartheid. If people made a full confession and admitted they were wrong, they would be forgiven and would avoid imprisonment. If not, they would face long prison sentences.

Mrs Mohapi, the first witness before the Truth and Reconciliation Commission (TRC), is sworn in on 15 April 1996. She gave testimony relating to her husband's death while he was in prison.

It was hoped that the TRC would help people like Steve Biko's family. The past would be brought to light, openly admitted, and then people could move on. The idea was to create an atmosphere that would allow black and white South Africans to build a new society together.

Painful truths

The TRC lasted for 2 years and heard evidence from thousands of people. The families of victims, victims who had survived, and those who had killed black people appeared in public and stated their cases. There were many emotional moments, especially when black people came face to face with those who had murdered members of their family. Many white people were shocked to discover what had happened. Some people broke down when confessing what they had done and asked for forgiveness. Many black people accepted pleas for forgiveness, but some found it impossible to do so.

Did it work?

Some people felt that the TRC let guilty people off too lightly. Members of the racist government did not accept any personal responsibility for what had happened. Individual policemen were blamed and politicians claimed they had not given permission for black people to be tortured and killed.

The TRC did set a worthwhile example for the rest of the world. A record of acts of injustice were admitted and made public. Records of what happened have been written down and recorded on film. People in the future will know about the past. The TRC tried to help prepare all South Africans to live together without denying the past.

Steve Biko makes a speech in the early 1970s. He later died at the hands of the South-African police,

The Truth and Reconciliation Commission

Date: 1996–1998
Where: various locations around South Africa
Statements taken: over 20,000
Statements taken in public: 2,000
Negative response: P. W. Botha, former president of South Africa, called it "a witch-hunt"
Positive response: Cynthia Ngewu said, "If it means that the policeman who killed my son becomes human again, and that all of us get our humanity back, then I support the whole Commission".

Peace in Northern Ireland

By 1990, a violent conflict had been tearing Northern Ireland apart for over twenty years. The problem went back further, to the 1920s, when most of Ireland gained its independence, but a region in the north remained part of the UK. The majority of people in Northern Ireland were **Protestants**, most of which were **Unionists** and wanted to stay part of the UK. **Catholics** were the minority, and most of them were **Republicans** that wanted Northern Ireland to break from the UK and join the rest of Ireland. The Protestants held power, treating the Catholic minority as second-class citizens. Trouble started in 1968 when the Protestant government refused the demands of Catholics for equal **civil rights**. This developed into a violent conflict. The Irish Republican Army (**IRA**) began fighting for Northern Ireland to separate from the UK and to join with the rest of Ireland. Protestant **extremists** began fighting to stay part of the UK.

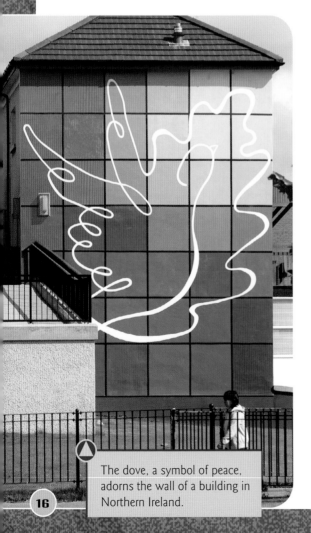

The dove, a symbol of peace, adorns the wall of a building in Northern Ireland.

A ceasefire

By 1994, it was clear that fighting in Northern Ireland between the IRA and **security forces** from the UK was not solving anything. The IRA had its own political party, **Sinn Féin**, which said that it was prepared to begin peace talks with the UK. The main Protestant party in Northern Ireland, the Unionists, and the UK government were also willing to talk peace terms.

Many millions of people in the United States are descended from Irish immigrants. In 1994, when the IRA declared a **ceasefire**, a US influence was brought into the peace talks. US Senator George Mitchell was invited to meet the two sides for talks and things looked hopeful.

In 1996, the IRA decided that the UK government was delaying the peace talks and preventing a settlement. They exploded a large bomb in London, killing two people, and the ceasefire was over.

Peace – almost

In 1997, a new British government took power and talks with Sinn Féin began once more. The result of these talks was the **Good Friday Agreement** in 1998. The IRA agreed to put their weapons out of use and a new government was set up in Northern Ireland – one that fairly represented both Catholics and Protestants. Sinn Féin would be part of this government and would continue to campaign peacefully for a united Ireland.

It was almost peace. One section of the IRA would not accept the deal because the Good Friday Agreement did not immediately bring about a united Ireland. In 1998, they planted a bomb in the county of Omagh and 29 people were killed. Protestant extremists also refused to accept the Good Friday Agreement because they did not want to share the power they had always held in Northern Ireland. This caused a problem – these extremists were represented in the new Northern Ireland government and they would not work with Sinn Féin.

A terrified Catholic girl is shielded by her mother and police officers in riot gear on her way to school, in the midst of violent Protestant demonstrations in North Belfast.

Northern Ireland today

In July 2001, the UK government suspended the new Northern Ireland government. This was because Protestant politicians, opposed to the Good Friday Agreement, made the government impossible. Important changes continued, including the formation of a new police force that was not seen as representing just the Protestants. Sinn Féin continues to campaign, peacefully, for a united Ireland, and a new government in Northern Ireland is likely to emerge in the future.

Russia after the Cold War

The Cold War came to an end in the late 1980s. The USSR itself broke up and Russia became an independent country. Under its new leader, Boris Yeltsin, Russia began getting rid of its communist system. This meant that many industries and factories that had belonged to the government would become private businesses that could be bought and sold. The government would no longer fix the price of goods and these would go up or down according to supply and demand. Under the new capitalist system there would be far more economic freedom, and people could buy and sell anything they wanted. It also meant, however, that people no longer had guaranteed employment, inexpensive housing, or free medical care.

Paying the price

The early 1990s was a period of tremendous change and shock for ordinary Russians. Prices went up, people lost their life savings because everything was more expensive, unemployment increased, and there was a lot of disagreement about how the Russian economy and society should be organized. People lost confidence in the future and poverty became widespread. Yeltsin was expected to lose the 1996 election.

Yeltsin made a deal with rich businessmen. He said that after the election he would sell them valuable industries that belonged to the government. In return, banks and businesses supported his election campaign with large amounts of money. Newspaper and television stations also supported him, and he just managed to win the election. It was good news to those who were benefiting from the new system, but a disappointment to those who were suffering. Supporters of the communist system felt that Russia – once a superpower – had now been humiliated by the **West**. They blamed Yeltsin for allowing this to happen.

A huge crowd of communist, anti-Yeltsin demonstrators gather outside the Russian White House in Moscow, Russia, March 1993.

Time to change

By the late 1990s, most Russians were still poor while a small number had become extremely rich. The country was very **corrupt**, with the government doing deals with businessmen, and the economy was suffering. There were large protests against Yeltsin and he decided to retire as leader. In 1999, Vladimir Putin became the new leader of Russia.

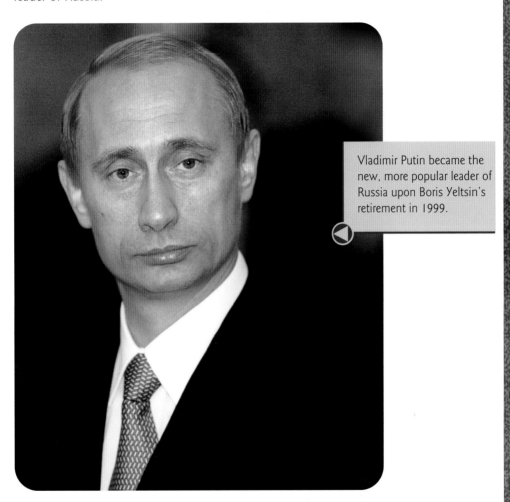

Vladimir Putin became the new, more popular leader of Russia upon Boris Yeltsin's retirement in 1999.

Russia under Putin

Putin became a popular leader in Russia. This was mainly because he did not continue with the kind of policies that earned Yeltsin a bad name. Putin promised to put a stop to people becoming extremely rich at the expense of ordinary Russians. Just as importantly, he wanted to return to Russians a sense of self-respect and pride in their country. This was something they felt they had lost under Yeltsin.

World problems

In the 1990s, the killer disease, AIDS, became a world wide problem. At the same time, huge problems were arising from illegal trade in drugs, and the disease, tuberculosis, was making a deadly comeback.

The AIDS memorial quilt, being displayed under the Washington Monument, Washington D.C., United States, October 1992. The quilt is made of more than 38,000 panels, each commemorating a victim of AIDS.

AIDS

The symptoms of acquired immuno-deficiency syndrome (AIDS) were being felt by people all over the world in the 1970s and 1980s. The United States was first to name the disease in 1981. Australia identified its first AIDS case in 1983. By the early 1990s, AIDS had become a worldwide **epidemic**. Sufferers suddenly developed rare cancers, suffered severely from lots of virus infections, which they were unable to shake off, grew steadily more ill, and died. In 1983, scientists discovered the virus that causes AIDS. They named it Human Immunodeficiency Virus (HIV). It attacks people's immune system – the part of our bodies that fights infection – and sufferers have no way of protecting themselves against even common illnesses, like a cold or flu.

Finding a cure

Scientists began looking for a cure to help people with the virus, or a **vaccine** to stop people from catching it. It was discovered that the virus was spread by sexual contact or by sharing used **hypodermic** needles. In the early 1980s, some people had contracted the disease from **transfusions** of blood that was infected. Doctors at the time did not realize that the disease could be caught in this way, and they did not test blood donations for the virus. In the 1990s, drugs were discovered that could slow down the effects of the virus, but no vaccine or cure was found. Meanwhile, the virus spread across the United States, western Europe, and Africa and began to infect people in Asia and eastern Europe. There is still no known cure for AIDS.

Tuberculosis

Until the 1950s, tuberculosis (TB), a lung disease, had been a major killer. In some cities it killed as many as one in six people. In 1942, a cure was found for the infection. This cure was an **antibiotic** called streptomycin. Doctors hoped that eventually TB might disappear from the world. In the 1980s, however, there was an increase in the number of people with the disease and many of them were found to have a variety of the disease that could not be cured by streptomycin. In countries with only basic medical treatment programmes the disease began to spread. In 1993, the **World Health Organization** declared a worldwide emergency because of outbreaks of TB. At present there are 40 million known cases of TB worldwide, and 2–3 million people still die from the disease every year.

This graph shows the decrease in the world death rate from tuberculosis since 1900.

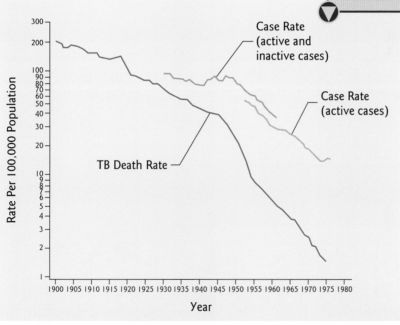

The drugs trade

By the 1990s, heroin and cocaine were widely used in many countries around the world. These drugs are highly addictive. They caused hundreds of deaths and were leading to an increase in robberies, as people needed money to pay for them. These drugs were ruining the lives of the people who became caught up in them. The trade in these drugs from countries in South America and Asia was illegal, but highly profitable. By the early 1990s, the illegal drugs trade had become the most profitable business in the world. It was earning up to US$500 billion a year.

ART AND ENTERTAINMENT

In the UK a new kind of art and music was emerging in the 1990s. In music, new bands such as Oasis, Blur, and Pulp were releasing hit records that were popular all over the world. Artists such as Damien Hirst and Tracey Emin displayed types of art that had never been seen before. They were praised by some and laughed at by others. Some new music bands, such as the Spice Girls and Boyzone, were also criticised and dismissed by some as "bubblegum bands." This meant business people in the music industry put these bands together simply to make money. Despite this, they became internationally famous.

New art

In the world of art, a new breed of young artists was receiving lots of attention. In 1991, Damien Hirst showed a dead shark in a tank of preserving fluid, called formaldehyde, as a piece of art. Other artists similarly took everyday objects and put them in strange places or made them look different. In 1992, US sculptor Jeff Koons made a giant puppy out of tens of thousands of flowers and plants. He recreated this popular sculpture several times in locations throughout the world. Others created very large sculptures. Louise Bourgeois, for example, created a giant spider with a cluster of eggs for the Tate Modern art gallery in London.

Carrying on from ideas of the 1960s and 1970s, a form of art known as "**installation art**" became popular. Instead of a picture that could be hung on a wall in a gallery, installation artists collected or made items that were then arranged by them to make a work of art. Tracey Emin, an artist from the UK, arranged an unmade bed and displayed it in a gallery. Photography, used in new ways, was also an important medium during this period. In one series, U.S. photographer Cindy Sherman from New Jersey, now living and working in New York, took photos of herself posed as historical figures. Others used new media such as video to make video art.

Nr. 224, a photograph by the American photographer Cindy Sherman from 1992, shows her as an historic figure from Roman times.

Usable art

Many ordinary people wanted to decorate their homes with new art for the 1990s. Designers responded with ideas that combined practical items with an artistic sense of fun. A metallic lemon squeezer, designed by French designer Philippe Starck, was made to look like a spider-shaped life form from outer space. This kind of item could be **mass-produced**, so that ordinary people could afford to buy it, but it still looked like a piece of art. In a similar way, a design company made a colander (for draining vegetables) that looked like a cabbage. Stores such as Ikea and Crate and Barrel produced everything for the home from whole kitchens, to candlesticks and toilet roll holders.

Antony Gormley

Antony Gormley is a UK artist who has won many prizes for his work around the world. Many of his sculptures involve models of his own body that he covers in plaster to make a mould. In 1997, Gormley and a team of creators started to make the larger-than-life figure, *The Angel of the North*. This is a 20-metre (65-feet) high steel figure with outstretched arms, which stands on a hillside in the north of England.

Anthony Gormley's huge sculpture, *The Angel of the North*, dominates a hillside in Gateshead in the north of England, UK.

New architecture

The end of the 20th century saw a new wave of building design. New computer graphics were able to show designs from every angle. This allowed architects to experiment more, making more interesting looking buildings and finding ways of linking the inside and outside of buildings more creatively.

Revealing buildings

In a style called hi-tech, architects played with the idea of showing, on the outsides of buildings, how they were held up and made. By the 1990s, this way of thinking was developed into reality with buildings such as the Millennium Dome in London (1999). Designed by UK architect Richard Rogers, it was a huge fibreglass tent, supported by 12 100-metre (328-feet) high steel masts, and its design was visible from miles away.

In Vienna, the Haas Haus (1990), a building designed by the Austrian Hans Hollein, was designed to show, on its outside, walls of glass alongside walls of stone. The mixture of old and new surfaces reflected the past and future history of the city.

In Los Angeles, architect Richard Meier created the Getty Center (1997). Dedicated to art and culture, it contains pavilions and gardens, and its design works in visual harmony with its natural surroundings.

Taller and taller

Tall city buildings have always been seen as a show of wealth and power. By the 1990s, technology was making it possible for skyscrapers to reach higher into the sky than ever before. For 22 years, the Sears Tower in Chicago, United States, had held the record as the world's tallest building, but this was about to change. Asian countries that were once poor, but were now wealthy, wanted to show their sense of achievement. In 1996, the Petronas Towers in Kuala Lumpur, Malaysia, became the tallest building in the world. The two towers of the building are covered in steel and glass and are joined at the 41st and 42nd storey by a skybridge.

The Petronas Towers (left) and the Menara Marx's building overlook Kuala Lumpur City Center Park.

Smaller and more curious

Other architects built small buildings, but broke away completely from traditional designs. Frank Gehry designed the Guggenheim Museum in Bilbao, Spain, in 1997, to look like a mixture of high-tech building and nature. Curved walls spring out of the centre like the leaves of a living metal plant. Polish-born architect Daniel Libeskind's Berlin Jewish Museum (1999) was built in the shape of a bolt of lightning zig-zagging around an empty space. Like the Guggenheim, its walls are covered in shining titanium. The unfilled space represents Berlin's missing Jewish community. Many of Germany's Jews were murdered in the **Holocaust** during the Second World War.

The exterior of the Berlin Jewish Museum, built in Berlin, Germany, in 1999.

Architectural feats

Two airports built during the 1990s reflected the amazing new technology in building. Renzo Piano built Kansai Airport in Japan on a man-made island, linked to the mainland by a 3-kilometre (1.8-mile) long bridge. A stunning steel and glass airport building sits on the island. In 1998, Hong Kong's new international airport opened. Built on an extension to an island off Hong Kong, it is also linked to the mainland by a huge suspension bridge.

The digital decade

Computers had become possible after the discovery that all information could be made into a series of **binary** codes using just the digits 0 and 1. In electronic terms, the 1 is a single pulse of electricity and the 0 is no pulse of electricity. Most of the technology of the 1990s was based on this binary code, called digital technology. Products such as washing machines, cameras, radios, telephones, televisions, and devices for recording sounds and pictures had all existed before the 1990s. What changed was the ability to produce versions of them that worked using digital technology.

Mobile phones

In the late 1980s, mobile telephones came on the market. The first models were large, heavy objects that were too expensive for most ordinary people to buy. In the United States they were mainly used as car phones and were installed into the arm rests of car seats. During the 1990s, the technology developed quickly. In about 10 years the weight of mobile phones was reduced by 80 per cent. New models became programmable, and could memorise phone numbers, record messages, send text messages, and much more.

The price of mobile phones fell and more and more people began to use them. In 1997, Finland became the first country in the world to have more mobile phones than ordinary landline telephones. By 2000, more than half the people in the UK and 29 per cent of the adult population of the United States had mobile phones. As new functions were introduced and phones became smaller, older mobile phones became less fashionable.

The most complete range of truly hand portable phones from International Communications.

An early Vodafone advertisement for the first portable phones, which were slowly shrinking in size during the late 1980s.

Screen technology

By 2000, there were 100 times more screens than there had been in 1990. Screens of various sizes had become part of everyday life. As well as being part of computers and digital cameras, they appeared in football stadiums, on the flight decks of aeroplanes, in hospital medical equipment, at airports, railway stations, supermarket checkouts, and on mobile phones. Old screens had to be large and bulky because they needed large glass tubes to carry the images to the inside of the screen. By 2000, liquid-crystal-display (LCD) screens, which are much thinner, were replacing these. They contain tiny crystals that allow light to pass through or to be blocked, according to the electrical signal they receive.

By 2001, it had become possible to imagine a time when the traditional television would only be on show in museums. Visitors would wonder how people lived with such bulky machines in their living rooms.

This is a liquid-crystal-display (LCD) television screen, which is able to be much thinner than the bulky televisions of the previous decades.

DVDs

In the 1980s, many people owned video recorders. The problem with videos is that over time, the tapes wear out and the picture quality becomes fuzzy. In the 1990s, the technology was available to create digital video recorders that recorded pictures on to a disc. By 1997, these were on the market around the world. By 1999, recordable DVDs were affordable. Like fax machines before them, old style videos and video recorders were in danger of disappearing.

Music of the 1990s

In the United States, for much of the 1990s, pop charts were dominated by gangsta rap music and Grunge sounds. Towards the end of the decade a series of boy bands, such as the Backstreet Boys, 'N Sync, and 98 Degrees, came on the scene. These bands included choreographed dance routines in their performances. They were followed by a series of female acts, including Britney Spears, Christina Aguilera, and Mandy Moore, who performed in the style of strong female artists such as Madonna.

Grunge

Grunge music developed in the 1980s from a mixture of punk rock and the local music of Seattle, Washington, in the north west of the United States. At first, Grunge was not part of the mainstream music scene. It was not played on the more popular radio stations, and it had not spread internationally.

People who liked the music developed their own style of dressing. They wore baggy torn jeans and checked shirts. Like the earlier punk style, Grunge dress was a reaction against what was seen as respectable and conventional. It was the opposite of smart suits and designer-label clothes.

Madonna performs for a sold-out audience in Florida, United States, August 2001. Many still see Madonna, who began in the early 1980s, as the queen of pop music.

By 1991, Grunge bands such as Nirvana were getting their music into the charts. However, the suicide of Kurt Cobain, the lead singer of Nirvana, in 1994 came to represent the end of Grunge. Bands continued to play music that was recognizable as Grunge into the late 1990s, but the energy had gone from this style of music.

Gangsta rap, or West Coast rap, became very popular in the early years of the 1990s. It used the same style of rhythmic talking as Hip-Hop, but it was more violent and **explicit**. To some people it seemed to be too concerned with violence and some people accused it of promoting old-fashioned attitudes towards women. The most popular of these rappers were Ice Cube, Eazy-E, Dr. Dre, and Snoop Doggy Dogg. Gangsta rap soon became popular and a big part of the mainstream music scene.

House

In Europe, House music remained popular throughout the 1990s. This was rhythm-based dance music, and it was often played at large gatherings called raves that were arranged at short notice. At first it was not part of mainstream popular music but, like Grunge, it gradually become more widely listened to. By 1997, House and its more underground version Garage were being softened and made more fashionable. In the United States this music was less popular and known as club music. Acts such as Chemical Brothers, Fat Boy Slim, Daft Punk, and The Crystal Method became popular.

Kurt Cobain

Born in 1967 in Washington State, United States, Kurt Cobain became the lead singer and guitarist of the grunge band Nirvana. This band was the driving force of Grunge music. As a teenager he had little interest in school, but paid all his attention to the local punk rock bands. Grunge music became a way of rejecting popular music and the big business that exploited it. After a while, however, Grunge itself became just as popular and Cobain came to resent the people who called themselves his fans, but did not understand what his music stood for. He had also struggled with drug addiction for many years and, in 1994, he was found dead from a shotgun wound with a suicide note beside him.

Kurt Cobain, lead singer of the Grunge band Nirvana, performs during the 1992 MTV Music Awards in Los Angeles, California. Two years later he was dead.

While violence was dividing many parts of the world, the UK was drawing closer to Europe as a member of the European Community (EC). In 1993, the EC was renamed the European Union (EU). People from the UK could travel and work anywhere in the EU and some **customs** regulations were abolished. Trips across the English Channel, to buy wine and cigarettes in France because they were less expensive, became very popular. Plans went forward for the EU to introduce a common currency, but the UK was reluctant to join this.

Yugoslavia breaks up

The European country called Yugoslavia contained different countries, including Serbia and Bosnia-Herzegovina, and each of these contained mixes of different nationalities including **Serbs** and **Croats**. The end of the Cold War helped bring about the break up of communist Yugoslavia, but this created problems. Conflicts developed because some nationalities wanted to create new countries without sharing power with other nationalities in the same country.

Ethnic groups
- Serbs and Montenegrins
- Croats
- Muslims
- Slovenes
- Macedonians
- Albanians
- Hungarians
- Bulgarians
- Romanians, Slavs

| 0 | 160 km |
| 0 | 100 miles |

Serbia and Bosnia

Serbia would not accept the idea of Bosnia becoming an independent country in 1992. One-third of Bosnians were Serbs, but the majority of people were Croats and Bosnian **Muslims**. The leader of Serbia, Slobodan Milosevic, was an extreme **nationalist**. He wanted to create a "Greater Serbia," a country that would include large parts of Bosnia, and he began arming Serbs in Bosnia.

This map shows the different ethnic divisions in Yugoslavia in 1991.

"Ethnic cleansing"

A **civil war** broke out in Bosnia and the Muslims were caught between the Serbs and the Croats, who both wanted their own, **ethnically** pure states. The process of killing people – Serbs killing Croats and Croats killing Serbs – in order to achieve this was called "ethnic cleansing."

By 1993, the Serbs controlled most of Bosnia. The **United Nations** (UN) and the European Community (EC) tried to create "safe areas". Unfortunately, they were not successful. Economic **sanctions** were applied to the new Yugoslavia that Milosevic had created. Other countries stopped trading and supplying goods, and this weakend his power. By 1995, Milosevic agreed to peace talks and an uneasy peace was agreed.

The end of Milosevic

The Serbs also controlled a region called Kosovo, which contained a large number of Albanians. From 1997, Milosevic began **persecuting** the Albanians in Kosovo. This time, fearing more "ethnic cleansing," action was taken in 1999 to stop it. NATO, a joint US-European organization, began bombing Milosevic's army and forced them out of Kosovo.

In 2000, Milosevic lost an election and public protests forced him to go into hiding. In 2001, he was arrested and put on trial by the International Court in The Hague for crimes of **genocide**.

Srebrenica

During the civil war in Bosnia all the ethnic groups committed terrible acts. In one case in 1995, Serb forces captured the town of Srebrenica, which was supposed to be a "safe area" for Muslims. Not enough was done by the United Nations to help the Muslims, and the Serbs gathered up and murdered around 8,000 Muslims.

Serb residents walk past a destroyed mosque in Srebrenica, 30 January 1996. The Muslim "safe area" fell to Serb forces in July 1995.

Genocide in Africa

Around the same time as ethnic conflict was tearing Bosnia apart, another genocide was taking place in Rwanda in central Africa. This time, the rest of the world did not realize what was happening and the mass killing was hardly reported at the time. Only afterwards was the full horror known around the world.

Rwanda was home to two ethnic groups: the Tutsis were the minority group and the Hutu the majority. In 1962, the country gained independence from Belgium and the Hutus were in power. By 1990, the Hutus were still unwilling to share government with the Tutsis and this led to conflict.

Genocide

Powerful Hutus began arming their people with large knives. They also began to plan the murder of all Tutsis and even the **moderate** Hutus who were willing to share power with the Tutsis. Special Hutu troops were trained to kill as many as 1,000 people in just 20 minutes. The genocide, which began in April 1994, lasted only 100 days, but it led to the deaths of about 500,000 people.

Hutu troops practice marching with pretend wooden rifles on the road from Goma to Kigali in Rwanda, 1994.

Who was to blame?

Belgium has received some of the blame for what happened. The Belgian government wanted to keep some influence in its former **colony** by remaining friendly with the Hutu government. In the early 1990s, Belgium secretly supplied Rwanda with weapons, military training, and money. Although Rwanda is a small country, it became the third largest importer of weapons in the whole of Africa. The huge number of weapons made it easier for the genocide to take place.

There were United Nations and Belgian soldiers in Rwanda, as well as French soldiers, just before the genocide started. Instead of trying to stop what was happening, the French and Belgian soldiers were ordered to help rescue their own citizens and then leave the country.

The UN also did nothing to help. They claimed there was a lack of information about what was happening. Other people said that nothing was done because powerful members of the UN had no economic interests in Rwanda that they wanted to protect. Tony Worthington, a UK politician, expressed his unhappiness at the way his country did nothing to help. He said that if half a million white people had died, instead of black people, then something might have been done.

Africa at war

The Rwandan genocide affected neighbouring countries. Over 2 million Hutu refugees, fearing revenge attacks, fled into Tanzania, Burundi, and Zaire. This led to a civil war in Zaire that lasted until 1997 when the country was renamed the Democratic Republic of Congo (DRC). The fighting spread and other countries became involved, including Angola, Zimbabwe, and Uganda. By this time the Rwandan genocide was forgotten as armies and politicians fought for control of the DRC. The country had precious minerals – mainly diamonds – that promised huge wealth to whoever gained control. It is thought that about 3 million people died in the fighting.

A small Hutu boy holds an intravenous (IV) bag for his parent, who lies dying of the disease cholera in one of the many refugee camps in Zaire.

War in Chechnya

Chechnya was a part of the old USSR. When the USSR broke up in 1991, Russia wanted to keep control of this region. Russians live there, but most Chechens are Muslim. They have been trying to free themselves from Russia since the nineteenth century.

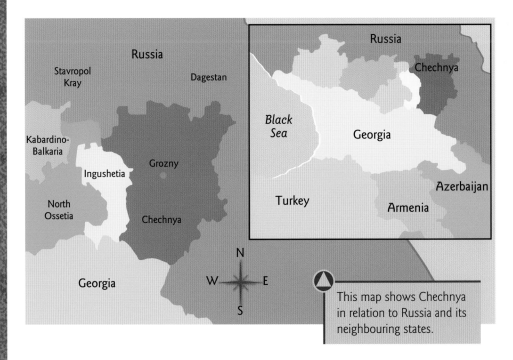

This map shows Chechnya in relation to Russia and its neighbouring states.

Chechnya demands independence

In the early 1990s, as Russia dealt with its own problems, Chechen nationalists began to demand independence. When Russia refused, a Chechen army was formed and thousands of Russians left Chechnya because they feared there would be violence. In October 1991, Chechnya declared itself independent. Russia withdrew economic aid and Chechnya became a lawless place, with ordinary Chechens having to manage as best they could.

Invasion

In 1994, Boris Yeltsin, the president of Russia, sent Russian troops into Chechnya to defeat rebels who wanted Chechnyan independence. The invasion turned into a brutal war and thousands of **civilians** as well as soldiers died. In the capital city of Grozny over the winter of 1994, 100,000 civilians, mostly Russians, were trapped without food or a proper water supply. Chechen rebels fought tanks in the narrow streets and around 1,000 Russian soldiers died in the invasion.

Grozny was finally captured in 1995, but a **guerrilla** war developed and the fighting continued. Various talks were held and peace treaties were discussed, but no solution was reached. It was estimated that 100,000 people died, and more than 400,000 people were forced to flee their homes during the 1990s in Chechnya.

Recent events

In 1999, a bomb exploded in the Russian capital, Moscow, and more explosions followed over the following two weeks. Chechen rebels were accused of planting the bombs. It is also claimed that secret agents working for the Russian government were responsible for the attacks. The truth is not known but, as a result of the bombings, President Putin began a second war against Chechnya. Since 1999, there have been further bomb attacks blamed on Chechen rebels.

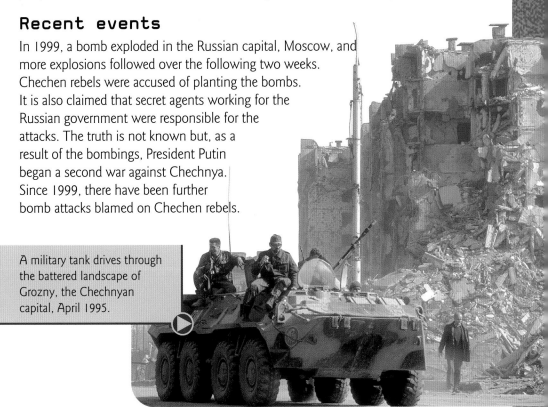

A military tank drives through the battered landscape of Grozny, the Chechnyan capital, April 1995.

People in Chechnya

"I have nowhere to go. All I have is my two children, nothing else. Everything I have is here."
Tany Yemelina, a Russian living in Grozny.

"We all lay on the floor, then went down to the bunker. I was in a bunker in 1942 [in the Second World War] and now again I am living in a bunker."
Gaslan Umarov, a Chechen who fought for the USSR in the Second World War.

"I don't know what they died for."
A Russian mother speaking of her son and other soldiers who died in the war against Chechnya.

(FROM CHECHNYA BY CARLOTTA GALL AND THOMAS DE WAAL)

The Palestinians

When the Jewish country of Israel was created in 1948, the Arab Muslim people who had always lived in that part of the **Middle East**, the Palestinians, were supposed to have their own country as well. Although this was the policy of the United Nations, it never happened. This was mainly because of a number of wars between Israel and neighbouring Arab countries. The wars resulted in Israel expanding its **territory** by occupying land that was originally supposed to be part of the country of Palestine.

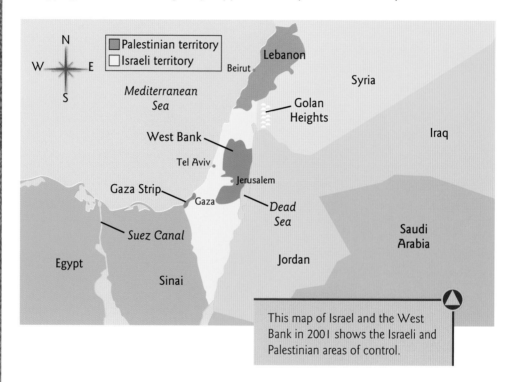

This map of Israel and the West Bank in 2001 shows the Israeli and Palestinian areas of control.

Adding to the problem was the fact that many thousands of Palestinians had left and been expelled from Israel. Many of these people had been driven out by Israeli forces, and others had fled because they feared persecution. They became **refugees** and settled in camps, where they still live, in neighbouring Arab countries. They still demand the right to return to their land.

Steps forwards and backwards

The Cold War did not help the Palestinians because the Middle East became a region where the United States and the USSR competed for influence. The United States supported Israel and the problem of the Palestinians was not dealt with. The end of the Cold War improved the prospects for Palestinians. However, Jews arrived from Russia to settle in Israel and many of them created settlements in Palestinian territory that was occupied by Israel.

In 1993, the United States helped bring Israeli and Palestinian leaders together, and some progress was made towards the creation of a Palestinian country. Israeli extremists objected to these talks and, in 1995, they **assassinated** the Israeli leader, Yitzhak Rabin. After this the situation got worse. Both Yasser Arafat, the leader of the Palestinians, and the Israelis could not agree on the boundaries and powers of a Palestinian country. Their talks came to an end.

The second intifada

In September 2000, the Palestinians began a second *intifada* (uprising). The first one, in 1987, had been based on **civil disobedience** and involved demonstrations and the non-payment of taxes. The second one used violence. As well as guerrilla attacks, a policy of suicide bombings was used. Arafat was no longer in control of the new Palestinian groups behind the second intifada. Many Palestinians had lost hope of achieving anything through the peace process and they began to support Hamas, the most important of these new groups. Hamas is fighting for an **Islamic** country of Palestine and believes that only violence will force Israel to treat the Palestinians fairly.

A bus burns after a car bomb exploded near Netanya, Israel, in September 2001. The Palestinian bomber was killed and nineteen civilians were wounded in the incident.

The Israeli government also used violence – in order to defeat Palestinian resistance. The result was that the suffering of the Palestinian people living under Israeli control got worse. Poverty and poor living conditions made their life more and more difficult. The areas where they lived became **ghettoes**, unemployment rose, and their freedom of movement was controlled by Israel. International aid organizations reported cases of malnutrition amongst poor Palestinian families unable to make a living. This situation continues today.

Palestinian refugees

As a result of Israeli military gains in 1948 and 1967, Palestinians are now scattered widely across the Middle East:

The Gaza Strip (area controlled partly by Israel): **445,000**
The West Bank (area controlled partly by Israel): **374,000**
Lebanon: **279,000**
Syria: **258,000**
Jordan: **846,000**

Total Palestinian refugee population: **2,202,000**.

Waco, Texas

In the United States in 1993, a **siege** took place at the headquarters of a religious **cult** called the Branch Davidians, led by David Koresh. The group had lived at these headquarters in Waco, Texas, since the 1960s. They lived a private life, believing that the world would come to an end in their lifetime. One of their ways of making a living was by assembling weapons from parts that they bought, and then selling them on. A US government agency, called the Bureau of Alcohol, Tobacco, and Firearms (ATF), made a raid on the building because the group was suspected of making weapons without a license. The raid turned into a gun battle, and four government agents and five Branch Davidians were killed. A siege began that lasted for 51 days. The FBI became involved and began negotiating with the leaders of the group to give themselves up. Inside, families were hiding in underground shelters away from the gunfire.

The Branch Davidian compound in Waco, Texas, United States, is engulfed by flames, ending the 51-day siege on 19 April 1993.

Oklahoma

In 1995, on the second anniversary of the siege at Waco, Timothy McVeigh, originally from Pendlestone, New York, and others planted a bomb made of fertilizer and fuel oil outside a government building in Oklahoma. The bomb killed 168 people, making it the worst terrorist attack on the United States up to that date. Within an hour of the attack, Timothy McVeigh had been arrested. He was found guilty of the crime and executed in June 2001. An accomplice, Terry Nichols was also later found guilty of murder.

The final assault

The FBI decided to break the siege by using tear gas that would force members of the group to leave their buildings. As people jumped out of windows and doorways to escape the gas, a fire broke out. Those who had not escaped were burned to death. Somewhere between 72 and 86 people died in the fire. Afterwards there was much talk about what started the fire and why it had not been put out. Critics of the FBI said that the CS gas had set fire, while others said that the deaths were part of a mass suicide. Firefighters were prevented from going into the site. The Branch Davidians that escaped the fire were charged with several offences, but many were found innocent.

Columbine High School

On 20 April 1999, two teenage school students went into Columbine High School carrying home-made bombs and a collection of guns. They wanted to blow up the school and planned for the bombs to explode at break-time, when most of the students would be in the school cafeteria. When the bombs failed to go off, the boys went into the cafeteria and started shooting. By noon they had killed fifteen students and teachers, and both boys committed suicide shortly after. Later, it was discovered that they had planned other attacks including hijacking an aeroplane and crashing it in New York. The shooting in Columbine added to the arguments in the United States about the way in which guns could be bought. Other people tried to blame the makers of violent computer games, which these boys played frequently.

Armed police surround Columbine High School, Colorado, United States, after the murderous shooting rampage of two of the school's students.

The UK, like other countries, made plans to celebrate the start of the 21st century. Similar celebrations had taken place at the end of 1899 to mark the beginning of the 20th century. There had been huge changes since then. There was far more equality between men and women and people lived longer. Working people had struggled for and won better working conditions, and a National Health Service had been set up. Technology had by now become a huge part of many peoples lives. However, there were also huge fears at the end of the century when people thought that everything with a microchip – computers, cars, airplanes, refrigerators, stoves, and clocks – would all stop working at midnight on 31 December 1999. This was known as the "millennium bug," but nothing ever did happen!

The environment

In the 1990s, more attention was paid to the effects of modern industry on the environment. The term **global warming** was used to describe an important change that was taking place around the world. Scientists detected long-term changes in the weather, caused by the Earth's atmosphere heating up. Gases such as carbon dioxide and methane cause global warming. These gases are the by-products of many industrial processes. When released into the atmosphere, they form a layer around the planet that keeps in heat, rather like a greenhouse does, which is why it's known as "the greenhouse effect."

Huge rows of traffic, a major contributor to global warming, queue on Sukhumvit Avenue, Bangkok, Thailand in 1997.

If global warming is not slowed down, there is a danger that Earth's ice caps will melt and all this water will cause a rise in sea levels. This is already happening, and the consequences can be disastrous for communities living on land close to the sea.

Deforestation

In the 1990s, people also became aware of the damage caused by cutting down large areas of forest – a process called deforestation. Thousands of species of plant and animal life are threatened by deforestation. Forests also absorb carbon dioxide, one of the greenhouse gases. So cutting trees down and reducing the carbon dioxide they take in means that deforestation increases the rate of global warming.

Tiny amounts of vegetation grow back on deforested land in southern Oregon, United States.

The Kyoto Protocol

In 1997, the most heavily industrialized nations of the world met in Kyoto, Japan, to discuss the dangers created by "greenhouse gases." They agreed on the need to reduce the rate at which carbon dioxide is released into the atmosphere. Their agreement, called a protocol, was to look into changes that each of the countries could make, and then promise to make the changes. Unfortunately, the United States announced that it would not agree to the Protocol – this was a major setback. Australia also backed out.

Judging a century

What was important?

Like a train gathering speed, the pace of life in the 20th century quickened with each decade. The years between 1991 and 2001 were especially eventful ones, but this had a lot to do with the dramatic changes that took place in the previous decade. Taking the century as a whole, it is difficult to look back and pick out what will remain important. Will the Internet still be important in 30 years time, or will it be something that people look back on as old-fashioned? Is it possible that problems to do with the environment will become more important than issues about terrorism?

An American century?

World affairs are no longer dominated by Europe. The Cold War, which divided the world for nearly 50 years, came to an end as the Internet age was beginning. In many ways the 20th century has been an American century and the United States, with over 700 military bases in more than 130 countries, is now the world's superpower. It spends more on the military than the next twelve nations put together.

Globalization

Much of the world now shares a similar way of living and this is part of what is meant by globalization. Part of globalization is that change can happen very quickly, because of modern technology. If something happens in one corner of the world, no matter how remote, it is quickly filmed and televised to show people everywhere. As a result, almost anything that happens anywhere in the world can produce effects somewhere else. In one sense, the world has become a far smaller place than it was at the beginning of the 20th century. People talk about the world as a "global village."

Perhaps the world we live in today is more of a "global city." In 1900, most of the world's people lived in the countryside but, by 2001, nearly half of the world lived in cities. When large towns are also taken into account the percentage of people living in urban areas is even larger. Some cities, especially in China and South America, are huge in size. Mexico City had only 350,000 residents in 1900 and now it has more than 60 million.

Problems

As well as environmental problems affecting the planet, the world's rapid population growth may also be a major problem in the future. The division between the rich and the poor, which has always caused problems, is now a bigger problem and it is becoming more obvious as a result of globalization. Many of the world's poor have stayed poor, while the rich have become richer and grown in numbers.

El Augustino, a shanty town in Lima, Peru, was still in a dreadful state of poverty in the year 2000.

World statistics

These statistics show just how different life can be between poor and rich countries across the world:

World population	
1900	1,600 million people
1950	2,500 million people
2001	6,000 million people

Average life expectancy	
United States	76 years
UK	75 years
Ethiopia	41 years

Infant mortality	
Japan: in 2000	3 infants died for every 1,000 born
Bangladesh: in 2000	118 infants died for every 1,000 born

This is the vast built-up landscape of Mexico City, Mexico, as it appears at the beginning of the 21st century.

43

SEPTEMBER 11, 2001

September 11, 2001, began as a very ordinary day in the UK. Summer was over and students were back at school and college. The early morning and midday news slots on television and radio contained no dramatic stories. By 2 p.m., everything had changed. The regular programmes on television and radio were interrupted to bring alarming news from New York, United States. Live reports brought shocking pictures on to television screens. In Australia, it was night-time when similar pictures and reports kept everyone awake. In New York, it was early in the morning and the working day had just begun.

8:46 a.m.

An American Airlines flight from Boston to Los Angeles hits the north tower around the 94th to the 98th floor of the World Trade Center in New York, crashing through the walls and destroying the stairwells. The top floors burst into flames and the people inside are trapped. Below the crash site people begin to **evacuate** the building. Over the next hour and a half twenty people, faced with the certainty of being burnt alive, throw themselves out of the building to their deaths – one of them killing a policeman standing below. The people in the south tower are told to stay where they are because their building is not damaged.

9:02 a.m.

A second plane hits the south tower between floors 78 and 84. Burning fuel traps the people above the 84th floor. The people below the 78th floor begin evacuating the building.

9:37 a.m.

402 kilometres (250 miles) away, a third plane flies into the **Pentagon** building in Washington, D. C., hitting a block of mostly empty offices that burst into flames.

Hijacked United Airlines Flight 175 heads towards the World Trade Center, shortly before slamming into the south tower. The north tower burns following the earlier attack.

9:59 a.m.

The south tower of the World Trade Center collapses. Millions of people around the world watch this live on television, just as they had watched the second plane hit the south tower.

10:03 a.m.

A fourth plane crashes in Pennsylvania before it reaches its intended target in Washington.

10:15 a.m.

Part of the Pentagon collapses.

10:28 a.m.

The north tower of the World Trade Center collapses. By this time, fighter jets are covering the air space above New York and Washington with orders to shoot down any suspect planes that do not obey orders to land.

World Trade Center's south tower collapses to the ground after a huge fire, caused by the airplane bomb, blazes through the building.

7:00 p.m

Volunteer construction workers stand around the site in New York waiting to help in the search for survivors, and rows of ambulances stand ready to take the injured to hospital. There are few survivors. Relatives have begun posting pictures of the missing around the neighbouring streets.

7:45 p.m.

The New York Police Department announce that at least 78 officers are missing. The Fire department estimates that 200 firefighters may be dead.

The immediate response

By 9:45 a.m. all flights across the United States were grounded. The White House and the Capitol Building were closed down. At 10:45 a.m. mass evacuations of key buildings in New York and Washington, D.C. began. At 1:44 p.m. five warships and two aircraft carriers were sent out to protect the United State's east coast. Other anti-aircraft ships were put out to sea.

Background to 9/11

Following the United States style of writing dates, what happened on September 11 2001 became known around the world as 9/11. Four passenger aeroplanes had been hijacked and used as flying bombs. Some passengers and crew had been able to make phone calls from the planes and they reported that the hijackers had taken control of the planes using small box-cutter knives. There were 19 hijackers and they died along with all the passengers and crew of the four planes. A total of just under 3,000 people died as a result of 9/11.

Osama Bin Laden

By the afternoon of 11 September, Osama Bin Laden had been named as the chief suspect behind the attacks. He has since become the "most wanted man in the world," and the reward for information leading to his capture is US$25 million.

Osama Bin Laden was born in 1957 into an extremely rich Saudi Arabian family and was brought up as a strict Muslim. He went to Afghanistan to help fight the USSR, which had invaded the country in 1979. The fight against the USSR was supported by the United States. He set up Al-Qaeda in 1988. He returned to Saudi Arabia and criticised his country for allowing US troops to be stationed there and for supporting the United States in the Gulf War of 1991. He was forced to leave and went to Sudan. In the late 1990s, he went back to Afghanistan, when the country became an Islamic state under the rule of a religious government called the Taliban.

Al-Qaeda

The Al-Qaeda organization is violently opposed to the presence of US troops in Islamic countries. It sees this as an attack on Islamic culture. Al-Qaeda is also opposed to the United State's support of Israel, blaming the United States for the failure to create a Palestinian country. Before 9/11, Al-Qaeda organized a number of attacks on United States targets. These included the bombing of the US embassies in Tanzania and Kenya in 1998, and mounting a suicide attack on the USS *Cole* in Yemen in 2000.

Osama Bin Laden is leader of the Al-Qaeda terrorist organization.

Why did the towers collapse?

After being hit by the planes, the two towers of the World Trade Center were obviously damaged. Most people, however, including the firefighters, did not expect them to collapse so quickly. It was not widely known how the towers had been built. In order to deal with the problem of vibration from wind sway in such high buildings, solid concrete walls were not used. Instead, each tower was held up by 240 hollow steel columns. When a plane carrying thousands of gallons of fuel and travelling at around 966 kilometres (600 miles) per hour crashed into the buildings, intense fires began. The steel columns melted and brought down the towers.

The US Navy destroyer USS *Cole* is towed away from Aden, Yemen, into open sea on 29 October 2000, after an Al-Qaeda-operated suicide boat was driven into the ship.

Consequences of 9/11

At the start of the 20th century, the Wright brothers made the first successful flight of a powered aircraft at Kitty Hawk, North Carolina, United States. Nearly a hundred years later, and for the first time ever, almost all civilian air travel across the United States was suspended for three days as a consequence of 9/11.

At the start of the century, flying in a plane was an exciting sign of the times. At the start of the 21st century, the results of that technology had become a weapon in the hands of extremists. Flying in a plane only became safe after very careful security checks that included, for flights to and from the United States, plainclothes armed guards pretending to be passengers.

A "wanted" poster for Osama Bin Laden hangs next to the US flag in a store window in Manhattan, New York, the day after the terrorist attacks.

Grim statistics from 9/11

Number of nationalities accounting for those killed in the attacks: **115**
Number of people who lost a wife/husband/partner in the attacks: **1,609**
Estimated number of children who lost a parent: **3,051**
Tons of debris removed from site: **1,506,124**
Days the fires continued to burn after the attack: **99**
Total number of hate-crimes reported to the Council on American-Islamic Relations nationwide since 9/11: **1,714**
Number of Americans who changed their 2001 holiday travel plans from plane to train or car: **1.4 million**.

A sense of danger

Another consequence of 9/11 was that Americans became aware of a new sense of danger in their own country. The United States had been involved in many wars and violent conflicts throughout the 20th century, but these had always taken place in foreign countries. Now, for the first time, there was a sense that a war-like conflict was taking place in the United States itself.

As a result, the Patriot Act introduced new regulations designed to increase security. Some of these regulations have raised concerns about civil rights. The imprisonment, without trial, of suspected terrorists at Camp X-Ray in Guantanamo Bay, Cuba, is one of the main concerns.

Detainees in open air cells at Camp X-Ray in Guantanamo Bay, Cuba, are guarded by military police, February 2001.

"War on terrorism"

An immediate consequence of 9/11 was President George W. Bush's declaration of a "war on terrorism," and a hunt for Bin Laden and other members of Al-Qaeda. The United States asked the government of Afghanistan to **extradite** Bin Laden, but the Taliban government would only agree to transfer him to a Muslim country. They also talked about transferring him to a country such as Switzerland where, they said, a fair trial could be guaranteed. This never happened. The United States invaded Afghanistan later in 2001 and overthrew the Taliban, but Osama Bin Laden was not found.

TIMELINE

1990
Human Genome Project begins

1991
Chechnya declares independence from Russia

Grunge music gets into the United States charts

1992
Civil war breaks out in Bosnia

1993
Peace talks begin between Palestinians and Israelis

The Waco siege in the United States

World Health Organization declares a worldwide TB emergency

1994
Genocide in Rwanda where half a million people are murdered

First multiracial elections in South Africa

The IRA declares a ceasefire and peace talks begin with the UK government

Kansai Airport in Japan is opened

First Chechnya war begins

Suicide of Kurt Cobain

1995
About 8,000 Muslims are murdered in Srebrenica during the Bosnian civil war

Peace talks end civil war in Bosnia

Yitzhak Rabin is assassinated in Israel, and peace talks with Palestinians come to an end under a new Israeli government

Chechnya's capital, Grozny, is finally captued, but a guerilla war develops and fighting continues

A bomb in Oklahoma marks the worst terrorist attack on United States' soil to date

1996
Boris Yeltsin is re-elected president of Russia

Northern Ireland peace talks stall, and IRA ceasefire comes to an end with a bomb explosion in London

The Petronas Towers in Kuala Lumpur becomes the tallest building in the world

Dolly the sheep is cloned

End of first Chechnya war

Truth and Reconciliation Commission in South Africa

1997

Peace talks resume between the IRA
and a new UK Labour government
United States and Australia refuse to
take part in the Kyoto Protocol
Finland becomes the first country
to have more mobile phones
than landlines
DVDs become available worldwide

1998

The Good Friday Agreement
establishes a new Northern
Ireland government and an
IRA ceasefire
A splinter group in the IRA plants a
bomb in Omagh, Northern
Ireland, and 29 people are killed
Antony Gormley's *Angel of the
North* is erected

1999

Second multiracial elections in South
Africa
Anti-capitalist protest in Seattle,
Washington, attracts 75,000
demonstrators
NATO bombs Kosovo
Start of second Chechnya war
Columbine High School shootings

2000

Serbian leader, Milosevic, loses
election in Serbia
Start of second *intifada* (uprising)
in Israeli-occupied Palestinian
territory
Monkeys and pigs are successfully
cloned

2001

Terrorist attacks on New York and
Washington, D.C., known as
9/11 because they took place on
September 11
The new Northern Ireland
government is suspended by the
UK government
Milosevic is arrested and put on trial
for genocide
United States invade Afghanistan
Hong Kong international airport
is opened

FURTHER INFORMATION

Books

Columbine High School Shooting, Judy L. Hasday (Enslow, 2002)
Genetic Engineering: Debating the Benefits and Concerns, Karen Judson
    (Enslow, 2001)
Global Warming: Understanding the Debate, Kenneth Green (Enslow, 2002)
*Inside the World's Most Infamous Terrorist Organizations: Al-Qaeda: Osama Bin
    Laden's Army of Terrorists*, Phillip Marguilies (Rosen, 2003)
The Attacks on the Pentagon on September 11, 2001, Carolyn Gard, (Rosen, 2003)
The Attacks on the World Trade Center: February 26, 1993, and September 11, 2001,
    Carolyn Gard (Rosen, 2003)
20th Century Design: The 90s: Post Modernism and the Future, Hannah Ford,
    (Gareth Stevens Publishing, 2000)
20th Century Media: The 1990s: Electronic Media, Steve Parker, (Heinemann
    Library, 2002)
20th Century Science & Technology: 1990–2000: Electronic Age, Steve Parker
    (Heinemann Library, 2001)
Turning Points in History: Understanding DNA, Tony Allan, (Heinemann
    Library, 2002)

Websites

http://en.wikipedia.org/wiki/1990s
Encyclopedia with sections on the 1990s and the 2000s.

www.geocities.com/historygateway/1990.html
Weblinks to interesting sites relevant to history of women in Britain.

http://kclibrary.nhmccd.edu/decades.html
A history site dedicated to US history on a decade-by-decade basis.

http://history.evansville.net/modern.html
Lots of history links, including the Arab-Israeli conflict and the Middle East.

Disclaimer

All the internet addresses (URLs) given in this book were valid at the time of going to
press. However, due to the dynamic nature of the Internet, some addresses may have
changed, or sites may have ceased to exist since publication. While the author and
publishers regret any inconvenience this may cause readers, no responsibility for any
such changes can be accepted by either the author or the publishers.

the early 1990s to 2001

Books and literature	• *Harry Potter and the Philosopher's Stone*, by J.K.Rowling (1997), is the first story in the hugely popular Harry Potter series
Fads and fashions	• Buzz Lightyear, one of the heroes of the hit film *Toy Story*, causes a sensation in UK toy stores, Christmas 1996 • Girlpower takes over the charts as the Spice Girls have a string of chart hits from 1997
Historic events	• Hong Kong, a British colony since 1842, is passed back to China in a splendid farewell ceremony, July 1997 • Space landing craft *Pathfinder* sends over 16,000 images of Mars back to Earth • The turn of the new millennium brings huge celebrations across the world at midnight, 1999
Music, film, and theatre	• *The Lord of the Rings* film trilogy, directed by Peter Jackson, makes movie history. All three are filmed at the same time, win a total of seventeen Oscars, and *The Return of the King* is only the second movie in history (after *Titanic*) to earn over US$1 billion (a thousand million) worldwide
People	• Mother Teresa, the Roman Catholic nun who dedicated her life to working with the world's poorest people, dies in 1997, aged 87

GLOSSARY

AIDS acquired immuno deficiency syndrome – a fatal disease

antibiotic type of medicine

apartheid system of racial discrimination practiced in South Africa between 1948 and 1994

assassinate deliberately target and kill someone

binary way of representing numbers using only "0" and "1"

birth defect something wrong with a baby's health at the time of birth

capitalism economic system based on private ownership

Catholic Christian religious group

ceasefire decision to stop using weapons in a war situation

cell basic building block of life

civil disobedience breaking the law, peacefully, as a form of protest

civilian non-military citizen

civil rights basic rights for all citizens

civil war war between groups within the same country

clone exact copy of another living creature, gene, or cell

Cold War state of hostility that existed between the United States and the USSR between 1945 and the late 1980s

colony country ruled over by another country

communism economic system based on government ownership and spreading wealth

conservative member of the British political party, the Conservatives

corrupt not honest

Croats people from Croatia

cult system of worship based around one person or a group

customs border control

democratic system of government based on everyone's right to vote

DNA molecule containing coded information which can be transmitted through our genes

economy matters relating to money

empire control of countries by one powerful country

epidemic outbreak of a disease on a very large scale

ethnic to do with one race or cultural group

evacuate depart in an organized way

explicit very obvious

extremist group who in a conflict situation adopts an extreme position and refuses to back down

extradite send a suspect from one country to another for criminal trial

genes part of our body that carries information, like the colour of our eyes, which is inherited by our children

genocide deliberate and organized killing of a group of people with the intention of destroying their identity as an ethnic, cultural, or religious group

global warming increase of the Earth's temperature due to rising levels of the gas carbon dioxide

Good Friday Agreement agreement between the Northern Irish political parties and the governments of Britain and Ireland, which created a Northern Ireland Assembly responsible for many areas of government in Northern Ireland

guerrilla someone fighting against a government using irregular methods

Holocaust genocide carried out against Jews, homosexuals, gypsies, and other minority groups by Nazi Germany during the Second World War

hypodermic beneath the skin

infertile people who cannot have a baby naturally

inherit carry down from one generation to the next

Internet global network of interconnected computers

IRA Irish Republican Army, a military organization which until 1998 fought British governments because of the conflict in Northern Ireland

Islamic related to the religion of Islam

mass produced made in large quantities using modern industrial methods

Middle East mostly Arab countries located between Europe and Asia

moderate not extreme, willing to reach an agreement in a conflict situation

Muslim people whose religion is Islam

nationalist person with a strong belief in the value of their country

organ part of the body adapted for a vital function

Pentagon government office in Washington, housing the US Defence Department

persecute constantly attack (either verbally or physically) a victim

prefix group of letters placed at the beginning of a word, affecting its meaning

prosecute bring charges against someone in a court of law

Protestants members of the Protestant church, a Christian group

refugee person who has no home

Republican individuals or groups in Ireland who do not want British rule of Ireland

sanction applying pressure on a country or a group by refusing to trade with them

security forces forces such as the police and army who carry out the orders of a government

Serbs people who identify themselves as Serbians living in Serbia as well as Bosnia

siege trapping an enemy within a certain space and attacking from all sides

Sinn Fein Irish Republican political party whose main objective is to end British rule in Ireland

superpowers very powerful country with a lot of influence

territory land belonging to a group or country

transfusion (of blood) giving donated blood to someone who has lost blood through surgery or an accident

Unionist member of the Unionist political party in Northern Ireland

unique one of a kind

United Nations international organization of countries. Its role is to maintain international peace, good relations, and security.

USSR Union of Socialist Soviet Republics

vaccine something you are given to make you immune to a disease

West term referring to the way of life and government in Europe and North America

World Health Organization (WHO) international organization that monitors and reports on the health and medical systems of each country in the world

INDEX

Titles in the *Modern Eras Uncovered* series include:

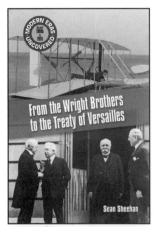

From the Wright Brothers to the Treaty of Versailles

Sean Sheehan

Hardback   1 844 43950 X

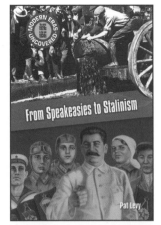

From Speakeasies to Stalinism

Pat Levy

Hardback   1 844 43951 8

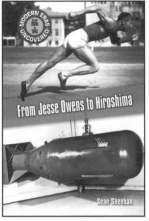

From Jesse Owens to Hiroshima

Sean Sheehan

Hardback   1 844 43952 6

From Television to the Berlin Wall

Pat Levy

Hardback   1 844 43953 4

From Beatlemania to Watergate

Sean Sheehan

Hardback   1 844 43955 0

From Punk Rock to Perestroika

Pat Levy

Hardback   1 844 43956 9

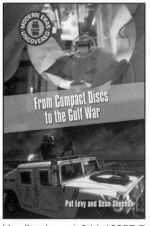

From Compact Discs to the Gulf War

Pat Levy and Sean Sheehan

Hardback   1 844 43957 7

From the World Wide Web to September 11

Pat Levy and Sean Sheehan

Hardback   1 844 43958 5

Find out about the other titles in this series on our website www.raintreepublishers.co.uk